FOR MY MOTHER AND FATHER. THIS COLLECTION OF WORK IS DEDICATED TO MY MOTHER, ROSEANN, AND FATHER, JACK, MY VERY BEST FRIENDS AND LIFE MENTORS. THEY FILLED ME WITH THEIR JOY AND LOVE OF LIFE, AND SELFLESSLY ENCOURAGED MY INDEPENDENCE AND CREATIVITY. EACH OF THESE ROOMS REFLECTS THEIR GIFTS TO ME AND WHAT HAS BROUGHT ME ARTISTIC SUCCESS—AND AN UNAPOLOGETIC FREEDOM TO BE AUTHENTIC.

JENNIFER POST MODERN

WRITTEN BY ANNA KASAB AN

POINTED LEAF PRESS

CONTENTS

MY WORLD

I am so pleased to have the opportunity to bring together this select group of design projects onto the pages of my second monograph, published by Pointed Leaf Press.

I have had the distinct pleasure in my career of working with an amazing cross-section of people—but each shares the same desire to have homes that reflect their essence while bringing them and their families comfort and joy. Many have become personal friends over the years and have called on me to design multiple properties.

Our successful collaborations come from a shared appreciation of the process that leads to perfection—an often-unpredictable path to arrive at design solutions that ultimately tell their stories and accommodate their lifestyles in unique ways.

Regardless of the locale or style, each of my clients looks to me to create an environment that pulls a curtain across the day and opens to a home where they can relax, recharge, and entertain with those they love.

For those who know my work, you will notice a design shift within these pages. Interiors are softer and more organic in shape, color, and fabric.

This shift comes coincidentally at a time when a more unpredictable world has us turning inward to our homes to escape and enables us to go off the radar.

These new interiors reflect the diverse ways this goal has been achieved—varied, intimate gathering places within the homes, cushily upholstered, body-hugging seating, more natural and stained woods, and bold pops of color that are meant to delight and surprise.

I always look to what is already in the environment inside and out, and to examine how best to honor that in design and interior architecture.

My focus is on keeping a calmness in my clients' spaces by replicating or recalling natural forms and hues that will envelope, and ultimately soothe the soul.

MY MANTRA, OF LESS IS MORE, REMAINS AS STRONG AS EVER. IT IS A MANTRA THAT IS LINKED TO MY EARLIEST EXPERIENCES OF GROWING UP ON 300 ACRES OF FARMLAND IT WAS THERE WHERE I WAS IMMERSED IN MOTHER NATURE'S PUREST COLOR PALETTES AND EXPOSED TO HER NATURAL SCULPTURES IN ROCK AND WOOD. IT IS WHERE I LEARNED THAT WE TRULY DO NOT NEED TO GILD THE LILY—WHERE CLEAN, OPEN VIEWS AND SIMPLE ELEGANCE MAKE THE MOST BEAUTIFUL ENVIRONMENTS. AS AN ADULT, MY TRAVELS AROUND THE WORLD HAVE FORTIFIED MY OBSESSION WITH THIS PURITY OF SPACE, AND CONTINUE TO THIS DAY TO INSPIRE MY DESIGN WORK.

HOME SWEET HOME

"I HAVE LOVED EVERY MINUTE LIVING IN THIS AMAZING BUILDING THESE PAST 20 YEARS AND WAS THRILLED WHEN MY APARTMENT BECAME AVAILABLE FOR PURCHASE. MY GOAL IN RENOVATING IT WAS TO CREATE A NEW, CLASSIC MODERN FEELING."

The transition from the outside to the inside at the Apthorp is haltingly dramatic. The landmarked 1908 building on Manhattan's Upper West Side, modeled after the Palazzo Pitti in Florence, Italy, is rich with detail. From the wrought-iron entry gate through to the gracious courtyard, it begs the question of what drew Jennifer here in the first place. After all, a modern glass high-rise would seem a more natural fit for her canvas.

"THIS CLEAN, ETHEREAL LOOK, WHICH HAS FOR SO LONG ATTRACTED CLIENTS TO ME, IS WHAT I NEEDED TO SURROUND MYSELF WITH, AS WELL. THE COMPLETION OF THIS HAS BEGUN A NEW CHAPTER IN MY LIFE."

Her answer is as concise as her interior architectural style. The Apthorp, she says, transitions her entry and exodus from the day and from the city's frenzied streets.

"...AND I LOVE THE GARDENS—I REALLY CAN'T LIVE WITHOUT GRASS AND TREES, AND THIS BEAUTIFUL COURTYARD, A TIMEPIECE IN ITS OWN RIGHT, GIVES ME THAT EVERY DAY AS I COME AND GO."

Her renovation was revealed in a theme of snow-white calm, with soft silk rugs, slabs of Bianco Dolomiti marble floors (her favorite of all marbles), Venetian white plaster walls, white lacquer cabinetry, and feather-light, billowing white yardage. Her move to modern though was respectful of the space's pre-war roots and translated via subtle details like her inclusion of high baseboards and classic nine-foot-high doors.

Room to room, views have unfolded with natural light now casting soft reflections and bathing the space in tones that clock the day.

"I PUT ALL OF MY DESIGN PASSION INTO MY HOME AND TOTALLY SPLURGED. IT WAS TIME."

Now when her frenetic days finally wrap up, moving past those stately iron gates is her cue that calm is a mere elevator ride away.

"MY HAPPIEST TIME COMES WHEN I LIGHT THE FIREPLACE, CURL UP WITH MY DOG ANNABELLE, AND MY CLASSICAL MUSIC MOVES THROUGH THE ROOMS."

PREVIOUS PAGES The inner courtyard at the Apthorp is a precious oasis of calm and offers a much-needed daily dose of nature for Jennifer.

OPPOSITE A sculpture by the English artist Lynn Chadwick floats atop a white lacquer credenza from Cappellini. The painting *Untitled 2013* is by the American artist Russell Sharon.

OVERLEAF Annabelle, Jennifer's adored Boston terrier, receives visitors in the foyer. Jennifer's Venetian plastered walls provide the perfect backdrop for her art collection. The painting, *Open No.18: In Ultramarine with White Line*, 1968, by the American artist Robert Motherwell, sits opposite a colorful canvas, *Untitled*, 2016, by the Costa Rica-based artist Federico Herrero. Two bronze hares by the Welsh sculptor Barry Flanagan in the distance break into the sea of white with a pronounced whimsical vertical energy. The rug is from Doris Leslie Blau, and the vase is by Robert Kuo. On the floor is a piece by the English sculptor Lynn Chadwick.

PREVIOUS PAGES Classic-contemporary furnishings address all of Jennifer's must-haves—comfort, warmth, elegance, and shapes—that are visually pleasing, stand-alone art forms. The lighting fixture was custom-made by David Weeks and the sofa is from Lazzoni.

ABOVE In Jennifer's redesign of the apartment, she removed the original high-detail period fireplace and replaced it with a more modern, sleek version.

OPPOSITE *L'Exile Noir*, 1969, by the Spanish artist Joan Miró, is reflected in an oversized mirror in the hall between the living room and dining room. A marble hippopotamus by the American crafts artist and ceramacist Judy McKenzie, which came from the Pritam & Eames gallery in East Hampton, New York, accentuates Jennifer's love of nature in this pristine space.

CENTURY

MEMORIES ARE CREATED
BY WHAT YOU DO TODAY

OPPOSITE Jennifer's study is a cozy space and has a pleasing view of the courtyard. She designed a series of built-ins without handles or knobs so as not to disrupt the clean look, and added warm yellow accents. The drawing is by the Swiss artist Alberto Giacometti.

ABOVE The all-white kitchen, by Bilotta Kitchen & Home, a Mamaroneck, New York-based company, is easily accessed by way of the glass-framed doors that open to the adjacent dining room. The portrait of Pablo Picasso is by the American photographer Arnold Newman.

PREVIOUS PAGES, ABOVE, AND OPPOSITE In the dining room, Jennifer placed the glass-topped dining table she designed with Paul Ferrante Inc. on a luxurious silk rug and introduced an earthy canvas by the Scottish painter, Callum Innes, from the Sean Kelly Gallery in New York, as the focal point. The trio of turn-of-the-century swans on the windowsill and the black Windsor chair, both of which belonged to her mother, hold special meaning for her.

PAGES 26–29 Her bedroom is the most ethereal room of all. The custom-made bed sits off the floor, hovering like a low cloud over a silk rug from Doris Leslie Blau. A dreamy sky-blue armchair from Rum Runner is tucked away from the sleeping area and plays off the same blue that is embroidered into the vines on her bedcover. Yards of soft white linen frame the windows and gently filter the light when drawn. This is a place where Jennifer can easily let go of the swirl of deadlines running through her life. The painting, *Untitled (blue)*, 2001, is by American artist Jacqueline Humphries.

COUNTRY BARN CHIC

"WITH THIS WAS A WONDERFUL COLLABORATION. THEY WERE VERY INVOLVED IN THE PROCESS AND OPEN TO SHARING WHO THEY WERE AND HOW THEY WANTED TO LIVE HERE."

From the exterior, the barn-inspired residence had all the architectural signals that could suggest a rustic, woodsy interior. But that was not to be for this Bridgehampton, New York, home. Part of a private family compound built by the Hamptons-based contractor Michael Davis, the barn-style look stopped at the front door. Enter Jennifer.

"A FAMILY MEMBER WHO KNEW MY WORK CALLED ME AND DESCRIBED HOW SHE ENVISIONED THE SPACE WORKING. SHE WANTED TO TAKE THE TRADITIONAL INTERIOR TO A NEW PLACE—ONE THAT WOULD BE LIGHT, CLEAN, AND MODERN … AND FUN IN ITS SPIRIT. IT WAS ALL ABOUT A SPACE THAT WOULD ACCOMMODATE A BIG, LOVING FAMILY WHOSE HOME IS ALWAYS OPEN TO FRIENDS AND FAMILY."

Among the alterations made to the architect's build-out was the creation of a double-height entry. The once-closed, traditional staircase received a major edit. Jennifer opened the stair treads, and replaced bannisters with glass. She also built out a glassed-in second-floor catwalk, adding drama and a dose of light. The original fireplace was rebuilt and turned into a sleek, modern focal point that frames a row of fiery flames running low across the living room wall.

"TO ACHIEVE THAT FEELING OF LIGHT AND OPENNESS MEANT I WOULD EDIT MUCH OF THE INTERIOR ARCHITECTURE. BECAUSE IT WAS SO THOUGHTFULLY SITED, I WAS ABLE TO TAKE ADVANTAGE OF THE NATURAL LIGHT THAT BATHED THE ROOMS, AND TAKE IN THE PLEASANT VIEWS."

Jennifer designed and furnished the main living room and den to welcome all generations coming together. For the living room, she included a huge, armless platform couch to accommodate a pile-up of friends and family. For anyone feeling left out, a swing provides a happy perch. The area is open to the kitchen and a banquette, but, as Jennifer notes, she wanted this area recognizably set off—but subtly so. She accomplished that by building a platform level.

"FIVE PEOPLE CAN LIE ON THIS TOGETHER AND WATCH TELEVISION, SHE SAYS OF THE PLATFORM COUCH. IT'S VERY INVITING, AND EVERYONE WANTS TO SIT THERE!"

A color palette of blue-on-blue tones and greys with a few pops of yellow, maintains the relationship with the outside, and complements the natural textures and colors of the surrounding landscape.

PREVIOUS PAGES Architecture that recalls a country barn wraps a modern, playful interior where comfort and joy rule the roost.

OPPOSITE Changing the height of the foyer allowed Jennifer to introduce a wonderful big, modern pivoting door for the new double-height space. Its clean-lined and warm-hued wood links the exterior to the interior. Jennifer felt that this, instead of the expected chandelier, was more appropriate, and set the tone for the unexpected design elements to come. The low double-pod bleached-maple bench, with a charcoal cast-concrete base, is the work of the American designer Mico Yektai of Sag Harbor, New York, recalls the kind of naturally formed "sculpture" one might come across while strolling through the woods

OPPOSITE AND ABOVE When Jennifer opened the stair treads and replaced the railings, she not only brought light into the space, but added something similar to an imaginative and dramatic art form.

OVERLEAF The anticipation of a living room filled with people of all ages to converse, warm up by the fire, and watch games on the television, inspired Jennifer's choice of furnishings. She opted for two sofa styles—both from Minotti—low in height, but roomy and upholstered in non-fussy, ultra-comfortable polyester fabrics. The armless platform daybed, from de Sede, which can easily hold a pile of friends looking to share popcorn or stories, is the most popular seating in the room. The small wooden side table is a custom-made design by Jennifer. The lighting fixture is by Douglas Fanning, in Brooklyn, New York. The hanging rattan chair is from Serena & Lily.

PREVIOUS PAGES Pops of color in the paintings by the Johannesburg, South Africa-based painter, Serge Alain Nitegeka, flank the main entry hall, and their black accents cleverly reference the stairwell's black bands. The elegant twin console tables are from Paul Ferrante Inc.

ABOVE AND OPPOSITE Jennifer's choices of an organic-shaped resin roundtable from Mecox Gardens, and a custom-commissioned, glass-topped oval table from the Brooklyn, New York-based designer and sculptor Eric Slayton, serve as perfect perches for snacks and drinks when friends gather in the main living space.

OVERLEAF The open space between the living room and the kitchen, from Bilotta Kitchen & Home, as well as the nearby dining area, with picture perfectly framed vistas of fields and trees, maintain the space's airy, casual vibe. Back-hugging bar stools from Roche Bobois welcome countertop dining. Jennifer's clustered seating arrangements, including a whimsical wicker swing, invite conversation. Her color mix of deep- to pale green–blues, lemon yellow, and tangerine speaks to the landscape's palette, no matter the season.

O'NEILL'S ROCK 'N' RO

ABOVE AND OPPOSITE Jennifer designed the powder-blue crescent-shaped banquette off the kitchen to face the beautiful landscaped views. It's a cozy spot for breakfast or lunch. The tangerine-colored abstract sculpture by American artist Almond Zigmund, from R.E. Steele Antiques, in East Hampton, New York, lifts our gaze out and upward, and recalls the deep tones of a summer sunrise or sunset.

OVERLEAF In the dining room, a custom-made table surrounded by 10 scoop-back chairs looks out to a mix of birches and tall bushes. Jennifer gave the room a dose of super calm with clean-lined furnishings. *Untitled*, 2018, by the English artist Mark Humphrey, offers a splash of warmth. The custom plaster wall was created by Kamp Studios in Brooklyn, New York. The candle holders are from the Comerford Collection in Bridgehampton, New York.

PAGES 50–51 Jennifer chose an L-shaped sectional from Baxter for the den and introduced an extra-large Holly Hunt coffee table to accommodate a crowd when the room is transformed into a movie-goers escape. Wall art by the American artist Michele Dragonetti adds color while suggesting that all who enter can sail off and enjoy.

THE BIG BOOK OF THE HAMPTONS

PREVIOUS PAGES Jennifer tucked the home office away into a quiet corner that offered expansive views to the property's plantings and gardens—all perhaps inspiration to complete tasks sooner rather than later. Low built-ins for storage leave the window views open. The outdoor furniture is from David Sutherland.

RIGHT The lower level of the home is devoted to a game room equipped with everything from ping pong, to pool, to television. To the right of the 11 Ravens custom-made pool table is a wine cellar. Jennifer chose plush, comfy furnishings, from Ligne Roset. Pops of apple red come in via low, S-backed tufted, ruched chairs that are perfect for a good read. The carpet is from Patterson Flynn & Martin.

11 RAVENS

ABOVE AND OPPOSITE The high-ceilinged master bedroom enjoys sweeping views of the manicured lawn and gardens. In preserving the calm a master bedroom deserves, the palest of blue-green hues were introduced by way of the wool rug, matching the Matouk bed linens, and art by the New York-based photographer Franz Walderdorff. Warm white draperies and shades frame the windows.

HOME

OPPOSITE Jennifer distinguished the children's bedrooms with simple design elements: The russet leather slats accent the young boy's bed, along with its hand-hooked "camper" pillow.

ABOVE The young daughter's canopy bed with built-in storage and a pink fabric-wrapped headboard make this room unquestionably feminine.

OVERLEAF The second-floor play area, down the hall from the children's bedrooms, allows for wall and rope climbing. The custom-built desk for two from Ducduc furniture welcomes board games and drawing, and a nearby tent serves as a cozy hideaway. Jennifer also introduced a big overstuffed chair from Paola Lenti as a great spot to relax in. The carpeting is from Patterson Flynn & Martin.

CARIBBEAN FREEDOM

When Jennifer's New York clients asked her to design an extension to their main house, she was very excited.

"UP UNTIL THEN IT HAD BEEN A DREAM OF MINE TO DESIGN A HOME IN THE CARIBBEAN, BUT THIS BEING A PRIVATE ISLAND, ONE OF A HANDFUL IN THE WORLD, AND ONE YOU CAN TRULY CALL A PARADISE—WELL, THAT PURITY OF PLACE WAS IMMENSELY INSPIRING—AN OPPORTUNITY FOR ME TO PRACTICE MY PASSION FOR CLEAN, PURE DESIGN ELEMENTS IN A LOCALE SURROUNDED BY THE ESSENCE OF IT."

It is said there are no rules there—freedom is the mantra. That resonates with the very core of Jennifer's design philosophy for this house, nestled into the hillside and down a stepping path from their main house.

"WHEN I FIRST CAME HERE, I SAT BY THE POOL AND THOUGHT HOW AM I GOING TO DESIGN THIS? I TOOK IN THE SURROUNDING VIEWS, THE SOUNDS, THE LIGHT, AND THE AIR. THE FAMILY COMES HERE FOR ALL OF THAT—TO LEAVE BEHIND THE DISRUPTIONS OF OUR MODERN, TECHNOLOGY-JAMMED LIFE. THAT MY CLIENTS PUT NO CONSTRAINTS ON MY CREATIVITY MADE THE ENTIRE PROCESS A JOY. SINCE THIS WAS OUR SECOND PROJECT TOGETHER, WE SHARE A MUTUAL TRUST AND ADMIRATION. THEY ARE GRACIOUS, AND SIMPLY WONDERFUL TO WORK WITH."

The open-air architecture welcomes endless views of sea and sky, and Jennifer's design strategy was to keep the inside-to-outside boundary transparent. Her choice of sea-glass colors in accent pillows—strung across the sofas—looks as though they had been tossed across a powdery white beach. In other areas, she introduced touches of coral in a floral fabric and in a woven screen playing off her clients' art and, no doubt, the coral reefs in the surrounding sea.

It is space that is designed for reading a good book, getting together for cocktails at the bar, drying off from a swim, or playing a game of pool. A sunken seating area, complete with an umbrella, was, she said, "just for fun," and the choice of coral accents frames the space and supports the convivial mood she wanted to achieve. "It's also a great place to come in from the rain," she added.

In honor of some of the island's most aesthetically pleasing creatures, she commissioned sculptures of 10- and 11-foot-high cranes and seagulls, as well as the turtles that are native to the island.

"THIS ISLAND IS BEAUTIFUL AND CALMING, AND UNTOUCHED BY THE NOISE OF THE WORLD—THERE IS AN ELEMENT OF FANTASY TO THAT, AND MY DESIGN FOR THIS HOUSE WAS TO KEEP THAT EVERPRESENT."

"I STOOD OUT ON THE BALCONY AND STRETCHED OUT MY ARMS AND LOOKED SKYWARD, AND THE IDEA OF FREEDOM CAME TO ME. I THOUGHT: THIS INTERIOR DESIGN WILL BE ALL ABOUT THE FREEDOM OF BEING HERE, THE PURITY OF THE ENVIRONMENT, AND THE PALETTE THAT MAKES IT SO."

PREVIOUS PAGES Having a design project in the Caribbean was on Jennifer's "must-have" list, as everything about island life speaks to her design senses and her passion for nature.

OPPOSITE The inspiration for designing the house for her clients came as she took in the view and observed the birds in flight to and from the shoreline. "It became so clear that, to be here," she said, "is to be free." Jennifer commissioned American sculptor Robert Hooke to create a piece depicting twin gulls in flight to keep that thought everpresent.

FOLLOWING PAGES Jennifer integrated tailored, slim-backed roll-away chaise lounges from McKinnon and Harris in clusters, creating gathering places with unobstructed views and silken sea breezes.

PREVIOUS PAGES Jennifer offered a respite from the sun by placing a half-moon sofa from McKinnon and Harris in the shade. White fabric with pops of sea glass-colored pillows dovetails perfectly with nature's palette, a color scheme that continues in the interior as well.

ABOVE Jennifer took every opportunity to frame the take-your-breath-away views and created vignettes as reminders that this is a place where embracing nature's beauty is the best reason to be there.

OPPOSITE In the foyer, Jennifer commissioned a duo of majestic cranes to decorate the custom-designed pool that welcomes visitors.

PAGES 72–75 A group of modular seating from J. Robert Scott comes together in front of the Palladian windows for a light-filled gathering place. Jennifer chose fabric that was close in color to the cool limestone-wrapped walls. She also re-introduced a few coral accents with pillows, a lacey carved screen, and a circular daybed from JANUS et Cie. Artist Douglas Fanning was commissioned to create the 11-foot-high aluminum palm trees.

PREVIOUS PAGES Jennifer distinguished another seating area with a soft fabric in a garden print. The two-tier coffee table recalls the gently rounded edges of lily pad leaves.

OPPOSITE AND ABOVE Her nature-themed thread moves through the space—as shown on the base of the table lamp, and on the custom-made console by Douglas Jennings. The woven wicker chair, with its flower-and-leaf–patterned printed pillows, is from JANUS et Cie

OVERLEAF For this corner of the house, Jennifer placed a group of colorful sofas and chairs from J. Robert Scott onto a stone platform to ensure that blue sky and sea wrapped all the views. Sky-blue club chairs offer cozy reading nooks and her choice of a printed coral fabric infuses this intimate little interior island with a burst of color.

PREVIOUS PAGES Jennifer created a whimsical focal point in this open sea of cream limestone and built a sunken seating arrangement that is evocative of the circles friends create on the beach.

OPPOSITE A suspended crescent-shaped chair welcomes barefoot beachgoers looking to cool down.

ABOVE Sea-glass blue accents for the bar area merge with the blues of sea and sky that make up the view. The limited color palette keeps the space tranquil and relaxing, and as elegant and timeless as a Tiffany gift box.

ABOVE The dreamy underwater scene by Orlanda Bloom adds a dramatic swath of color to the game area.

OPPOSITE A second two-step platform creates another, more private seating area. The sea-glass blues, greens, and coral theme continues, linking all the seating areas. The credenza is from Brett Design.

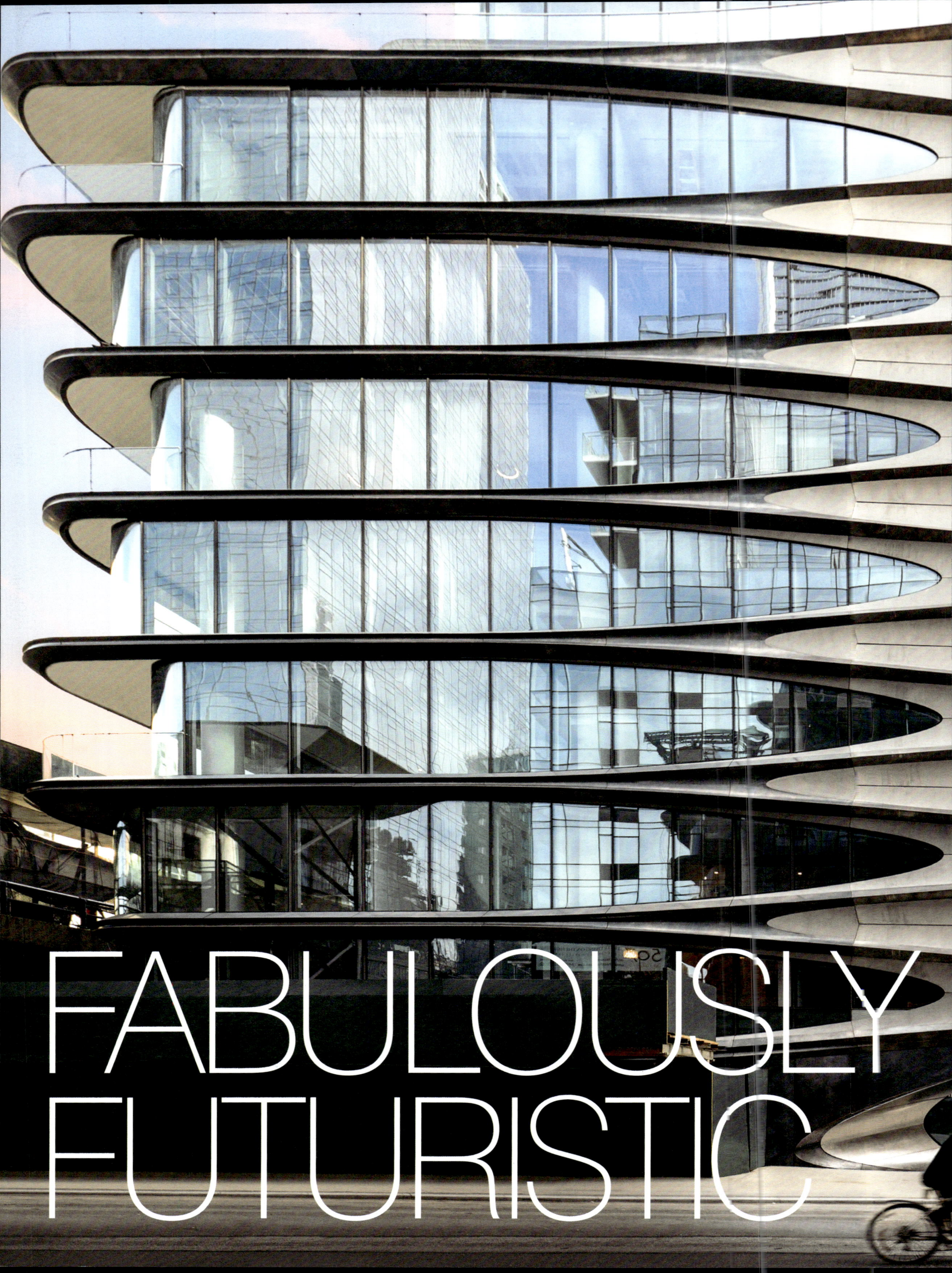

FABULOUSLY FUTURISTIC

"BEING INVITED TO DESIGN THE INTERIOR OF THIS CONDOMINIUM WAS ONE OF THE BIGGEST HONORS OF MY CAREER."

The creation of Zaha Hadid, it was the late Iraqi–British architect's first residential building in New York. The Related Companies, the developer, known in the United States as a pre-eminent builder of luxury properties, asked Jennifer to design one of the model units that has since been sold. Hadid, a Pritzker Architecture Prize-winning architect and often called the "queen of the curve," took her sculpting talents and gave the Chelsea neighborhood a work of art in glass and metal at 520 West 28th Street. With just 39 luxury two- to five-bedroom residences wrapped in a chevron pattern, Hadid framed the interior views in swirling bands of steel.

"IT WAS VERY IMPORTANT FOR ME TO TELL THE WORLD THAT HER RESIDENTIAL PROJECT, WHILE AS CUTTING EDGE AS THE EXTERIOR OF HER PUBLIC BUILDINGS, HAD ENORMOUS POTENTIAL TO HAVE INTERIORS THAT ARE APPROACHABLE, WARM ENVIRONMENTS YOU CAN CALL HOME. EVERYTHING I CHOSE FOR THIS MODEL HAD TO INSPIRE BUYERS ON THAT CONCEPT."

Zaha's crescent moons, ovals, and expanses of glass gave Jennifer many creative opportunities to echo graceful curves inside the four-bedroom apartment and simultaneously speak to comfort. For example, in the great room, she introduced a quartet of curved-back club chairs set around a low iron-based cafe-style table, an open-S chaise that mimics a window arch, and a trio of lozenge-shaped stools with curved bases. In the master bedroom, which was dominated by a massive oblong window, she introduced two cloud-like, gently curved chairs with pencil-thin wood bands that accentuate their sculpted forms. She placed all the furnishings atop a carpet with a repeating pattern of tiny ribbed curves.

The existing warm-toned wood floors supported her muted, earthy palette for furnishings and textural rugs. Pale green, bone, grey, sand, and cream are the hues that set the tone for a relaxed and inviting space. The few additions of yellow, coral, and blue move through the space like tasty design signals, taking visitors on a tour of an unforgettable space.

"OUR STYLES WERE ABLE TO MERGE IN A VERY NATURAL WAY. WHERE ZAHA HADID IS KNOWN AS A MODERN MINIMALIST, MY SIGNATURE STYLE IS LASER-FOCUSED ON CLEAN AND MODERN, AND HAS A MANTRA OF LESS IS MORE."

PREVIOUS PAGES Architect Zaha Hadid's swirls of steel snake around the residential low-rise at 520 West 28th Street in Manhattan's Chelsea neighborhood, presenting Jennifer with the coveted opportunity to design a space that merged a hard-edged, bold sculpture with a soft, warm interior.

OPPOSITE Jennifer's custom-built desk, attached to a wall of built-in cabinetry, took in the dramatic view of a wing of the residences' skyward climb. The swayback armchairs, from Fendi, echo the shapes in the view. Two square-lined soft leather guest chairs play off the linear shapes of the window frames and the square-on-square patterned rug. Jennifer's design is, as always, clean, restrained, and synergistic.

OVERLEAF With the living room and dining room combined in one large, window-wrapped space, Jennifer used clusters of furnishings to make the space inviting and intimate. The oversized ceramic penguin from Robert Kuo demarcates the seating areas. Jennifer devoted a third of the room to an L-shaped sofa that can easily accommodate a dozen or more guests, and added a trio of cushioned tub chairs for extra seating. Soft, earthy tones completed the look she was after—bringing inside some of the hues and tones of the outdoors. The ceiling and floor lighting is slim, sculptural, unobtrusive, and fitting to the serene mood.

ASIAN ART

PREVIOUS PAGES A snow-white pounded wrought-iron dining room table surrounded by 10 tailored, side-boxed chairs, has been tucked away against a floating wall. At right, a circle of club chairs around a low table provides yet another option for socializing.

RIGHT With Hadid's sculpted island taking the focus, Jennifer introduced lemon yellow stools to encourage conversation with the chef of the house. With backs that are thoughtfully lined up with the countertop, she kept the view open. The abstract sculpture on the counter is by the Canadian artist Martha Sturdy.

OVERLEAF The master bedroom offers perhaps the most dramatic contrast to the futuristic architecture. While Jennifer's choices do recall swirls and rounded edges, she has taken this room to a place of calm, with a subdued palette and ultra-soft-to-the-touch fabrics. She upholstered the Lazzoni bed frame and headboard in linen, and covered the bed with a down duvet from Ann Gish. The lounge chairs are from Bernhardt.

PAGES 100–101 The Carrara marble-wrapped master bath, an elegant ethereal space, begged for a piece of art, and Jennifer complied with the duel-figured sculpture *Double Kate Moss* by the British artist Marc Quinn, from the Opera Gallery in New York.

WORLD VIEW

"THEY LIVE IN AN ELEGANT COUNTRY MANOR ON SEVERAL ACRES. WHEREAS LIFE THERE IS CASUAL, THEY LOOKED TO ME TO TURN THIS INTO A REFINED CITY HOME."

Two days before Christmas, Jennifer received a call from the manager of one of Manhattan's newest ultra-luxury high-rise residential buildings, asking if she could please do an interior design consultation. As she was preparing to head home for the holidays, she was about to refuse, but once he explained what lovely people they were, a meeting came together.

"THEY WERE GRACIOUS, HAPPY PEOPLE AND WE IMMEDIATELY CONNECTED. THEY HAD JUST PURCHASED THE CONDOMINIUM A WEEK PRIOR. THE SPACE—AN ENTIRE FLOOR—WAS EMPTY, WITH EXPANSIVE WALLS OF GLASS AND VIEWS OF CENTRAL PARK, THE STATUE OF LIBERTY, AND LONG ISLAND. A MAGNIFICENT STORY WAS BEING TOLD OUTSIDE ... I WAS VERY INSPIRED."

Developed by the Extell Development Company and designed by world-renowned, Pritzker Architecture Award-winning French architect Christian de Portzamparc, the tower appears to thrust out of the Manhattan ground and push skyward, a dramatic 1,000 feet of glistening glass. Residents enjoy a building with services and amenities that cater to their every need. One of the first things Jennifer did to inspire and familiarize the clients with her work was to give them a tour of her own recently designed condominium at the Apthorp, on Manhattan's Upper West Side. A contract soon arrived, and Jennifer began drawing and pulling together sample material boards for their consideration.

"ALL THE MILLWORK WAS CUSTOM DESIGNED—EVERY DESK, DRESSER, BED, AND SEATING WAS UPHOLSTERED FOR ELEGANCE AND COMFORT. I CHOSE A COLOR PALETTE THAT PULLED IN THE CITY VIEWS—YELLOWS, BROWNS, AND GREYS. THERE ARE VERY FEW DRAPERIES, AS THIS IS A CELEBRATION OF CENTRAL PARK AS THE MAIN VISUAL."

One way Jennifer achieved elegance was by taking away the dark wood floors specified by the developer and replacing them with vast expanses of white marble. Once installed, the reflections of furnishings, sculptures, and the ever-changing hues of the sky played off the surfaces and set the tone. Jennifer replaced every door, opting for simplicity and visual quiet, and covered painted walls in Venetian plaster to soften all the natural light coming into the space.

"SOME CLIENTS USE THE CITY TO JUST COME IN AND PLAY; THEIR HOMES SERVE MORE AS A LOVELY STOPOVER. THIS FAMILY COMES HERE TO LIVE AND USE THE SPACE WITH THE SAME SINCERITY AND JOY THEY SHARE ON THEIR COUNTRY ESTATE. IT'S A PLACE TO RELAX, FOR MAKING GREAT FAMILY MEALS, AND TAKING IN THE CITY WHEN THE MOOD STRIKES."

PREVIOUS PAGES The spectacular sky-high penthouse with dreamy views of New York's historic landmarks gave Jennifer the inspiration to create a sophisticated, welcoming home. The coal-black sculpture *Standing Bronze #7* by Honolulu-based artist John Koga, from Ralph Pucci, plays off the hard-edged border of architecture in the mapped streetscape below.

OPPOSITE Always methodical in her design plan, Jennifer perfectly aligned the surface of the warm grey wood-topped table with its base, by the Brooklyn designer Douglas Fanning, with the window's band of steel—presenting a clean, unobstructed view. The twin diamond-shaped chandeliers are by the French designer Hervé Van der Straeten, and are also from Ralph Pucci.

OVERLEAF The foyer is a study in contrasts, with gleaming marble floors surrounded by warm tones in brass and metal, and sculptures that recall nature like this one by Hervé Van der Straeten. The console is by the French designer Eric Schmitt, also from Ralph Pucci. The painting is by Amy Morgenstern of Kamp Studios, in Brooklyn, New York.

PAGES 107–110 A plush crescent-shaped slate-grey sofa, by the American designer Vladimir Kagan from Holly Hunt, sits atop a pale grey ridged pile silk rug from Doris Leslie Blau, to create a comfortable space in which to entertain. The modular seating area is from Roche Bobois. A low metal and steel coffee table, shaped to recall lily pads, is by the Brooklyn-based designer Douglas Fanning.

ABOVE AND OPPOSITE A pair of brass and dark green chairs, with elegantly sculpted legs, by French designer Paul Mathieu, from Ralph Pucci, are tucked away from the main seating areas in a small office space. And as if one needed to be reminded of being sky-bound, Jennifer hung *EVA Air Boeing 747-400*, a print by the American photographer Jeffrey Milstein.

PAGES 118–121 Soft shades of grey allow the master bedroom to float into the sky-lit view. Touches of aqua in two canvases by American artist Karen Scharer, and on two contemporary recliners from Roche Bobois, balance a sophisticated, restrained, and elegant color palette. An arctic-white ceramic stoneware sculpture titled *Entwine,* by the Swedish-born artist Eva Hild, is like a cloud taken in the wind. The stone-grey upholstered bed from J. Robert Scott, sits high off the floor, ensuring the view will not be lost.

B-16709

ASPEN

BRANCUSI NEW YORK
ASSOULINE
ASPEN STYLE
ASSOULINE

OPPOSITE Touches of sea-glass green drop-lights, accented with silver metal bands, continue the subtle palette.

ABOVE The organic print from Hermès that covers the sofa in green and white recalls the canopy of the treetops in Central Park.

OVERLEAF Where the master bedroom focuses on cool, sophisticated tones, Jennifer chose a warmer palette of yellow hues for this guest bedroom. The diamond-cut linen tufts that wrap the headboard in pale yellow play off the shapes of the geometric sconces by the American architect Richard Meier.

1

ABOVE AND OPPOSITE The vanity in the master bathroom was designed to seemingly float above the city and appears carved from the marble below. The concept, per Jennifer, is elegance to the max.

OVERLEAF Jennifer saw no need to take the kitchen, by Wren Kitchens, a United Kingdom-based company, beyond shades of white and cream. Leaving it clean and simple in character, all the cabinetry is lacquered and spare, the drawer pulls are minimal, and the lighting recalls water drops. The mood is serene, while retaining the open feeling of the space. The hanging lamps are from Studio Italia.

ABOVE The kitchen has been furnished with the Ulu table designed by Jiun Ho New York. The base is cast in bronze and the top is white oak with a carbon finish. The Antoine chairs are by the British-born architect and furniture designer T.H. Robsjohn-Gibbings, from Dennis Miller, in New York. The sconce is by Richard Meier, and is from Ralph Pucci.

OPPOSITE Jennifer created another breakfast area in the kitchen by bringing together two swivel club chairs, and a sea-glass green table, all from Douglas Jennings. Her choice of a warm peach cotton continues the tangerine of the nearby stools, recalling the hues that come with sunrises and sunsets over Manhattan.

The Gardener's Garden

CLASSIC KAHN

Jennifer has had countless creative opportunities to work her design magic in some of the most notable residential projects in the country. But the commission to update the Korman House by the famed architect Louis Kahn was the first time she put her signature on such an important chapter in American architectural history.

Kahn, one of the 20th century's most influential architects, designed and built the two-story 6,950-square-foot Korman family home—a compelling series of connected squares and rectangles wrapped in glass, brick, cypress, Douglas fir, and white pine. It was the last house Kahn would build, and has been in the same family since its completion in 1973. Larry Korman, who grew up in the house and has been living there with his wife and children since the late 1990s, turned to Jennifer to bring the dated 1970s-era interior to a refreshed place.

"WHEN LARRY TOLD ME HE WANTED ME TO UPDATE THE INTERIORS, I WAS ECSTATIC. IT WAS NOT ONLY AN INCREDIBLE OPPORTUNITY, BUT ALSO AN HONOR. HE AND HIS FAMILY WERE A JOY TO WORK WITH. THEIR TRUST FREED ME TO TAKE THIS AMAZING HOME TO A NEW PLACE."

"MY APPROACH WAS TO RESPECT ALL THAT KAHN BROUGHT TO THE HOME AND ALIGN WHAT I DID WITH HIS CLASSICAL STANCE."

Jennifer maintained the integrity of his choices for consciously masculine, clean-lined, comfortable furnishings—all her custom designs—and a nature-focused palette that dovetailed with the surrounding landscape.

When Kahn was first asked to design the home, he posed the question to Larry's father, "How do you want to live your life?" A very specific answer came back that guided Kahn in every level of detail.

That list included a desire for simplicity and elegance, and an uncluttered look, exactly what Jennifer has done through her entire career, and which comes full circle in one of Kahn's most striking houses. The synergy between Kahn and Korman, and now Post, created a perfect collaboration.

PREVIOUS PAGES, OPPOSITE AND PAGES 144–145 The glass, brick, cypress, Douglas fir, and white pine house by the American architect Louis Kahn was completed for the Korman family in 1973.

OVERLEAF AND PAGES 138–139 Jennifer designed the living room with casual furnishings that afford the views center stage. The 11-foot-long sofa and green leather-covered swivel chairs are all from Minotti. The bench near the fireplace is from Walter Knoll; the rug, from Doris Leslie Blau. The dark oak coffee table was custom-made for the room. The stone sculptures are by Nico Yektai. The painting is by the American artist Elaine Kurtz.

ABOVE The custom-made table and banquette are embraced by the eastern sunlight.

OPPOSITE In the dining room, Minotti dining chairs surround a custom-made dark walnut wood table with a satin etched glass top.

OVERLEAF A silkscreen by the American Pop Art artist Andy Warhol, hangs above the bed, with its upholstered base, which came from Molteni. The plush, custom-made rug is from Tai Ping Carpets. The chocolate leather-covered Barcelona chair for Knoll is by the American-German architect Mies van der Rohe.

COOL & COZY

"AS SOON AS YOU WALK IN THE FRONT DOOR AND STEP ONTO THE HEMP RUG, YOU KNOW WHAT THIS HOME IS ALL ABOUT. THE EARTH TONES OF CREAM AND CAPPUCCINO BEGIN HERE AND ARE BLENDED THROUGHOUT THE ROOMS. IT IS THE PALETTE OF FALLEN LEAVES ON THE FOREST FLOOR, A DESIGN THAT RECALLS THAT FEELING OF QUIET."

This was the young couple's first home, a place where they looked forward to starting their family—and did—as a baby girl has graced their life since the three-bedroom home was completed.

The Manhattan condominium is in a new high-rise designed by the British architect Norman Foster. It offers eclectic city views of the Hudson River, Chelsea Piers, and a slew of brick-and-concrete buildings with rooftops that rise and fall in the big sky view like musical notes.

"THIS PROJECT GAVE ME A FABULOUS OPPORTUNITY TO TURN A DEVELOPER'S STARK THREE-BEDROOM SHELL INTO A WARM SPACE—A PLACE THAT EMBRACES NORMAL, EVERYDAY LIFE. THAT I INTRODUCED A NATURAL THEME—NATURAL FIBERS, ORGANIC COTTONS, LOTS OF WOOD, AND SOFT, PLUSH RUGS, RESONATED WITH THE HEALTH-CONSCIOUS COUPLE. I'VE GIVEN THEM AND THEIR NEW BABY A PRIVATE, ORGANIC COCOON."

White oak, stained to a soft grey, was chosen for the custom millwork in the den, his and her studies, and the living room. The white oak falls back in the view and softens all the linear edges. For the Venetian plaster walls—Jennifer's favorite reflective surface—she continued the warm theme by opting for a cream rather than snow-white tone.

Where art and furnishings can sometimes jump out at you, here, the concept was to gently ease you into every room. Sofas, chairs, and the ottoman are all softly angled, tufted, and cushioned for comfort.

"ONE ISN'T LEFT WONDERING WHICH ROOM TO ESCAPE TO FOR CALM. EACH IS IN ITS OWN RIGHT."

PREVIOUS PAGES AND OPPOSITE A soft-to-the-step hemp rug from Doris Leslie Blau serves as the pathway leading to all the rooms in this new Manhattan condominium, where Jennifer merged a palette of warm tones with elegant, clean-lined design elements. Her use of symmetry—as seen in the matching, floating consoles from Desiron—topped with matching lamps—sets a tone of tranquility. The, the mirrors are from Paul Ferrante Inc.

OVERLEAF As it was the young couple's first family home, where new members would no doubt be exploring, Jennifer focused on furnishings that are soft and comfortable, while upholding her mantra of clean and modern. Her sleek built-ins and shelving take advantage of an expanse of wall, offering multiple levels for displaying art and collectibles while adding warmth and texture.

PAGES 152–153 Low, ultra-contemporary arctic-white couches from Minotti sit atop a cushy silk white rug from Doris Leslie Blau. The magnificent river views are the focus of the room where one can enjoy reading on a sunny morning, and enjoy the view at dusk—when cocktails are served around the coffee table. Ultra-slim standing lamps, from Holly Hunt, cleverly tucked into the open corners of the couches, stay true to her design belief that symmetry and calm easily cohabit.

CHANEL
MODERN TIMES
YVES SAINT LAURENT

Berlin
Paris
London
Impressionist Art
Travel
THE GRAND TOUR

VISIONAIRE

PREVIOUS PAGES Jennifer's custom-made partners' desk is flanked by more than 15 feet of shelving and storage, all stained in soft grey, which extends to the city sky and rooftop views. The linear theme from built-ins to the desk, along with the restrained palette, sustain the peaceful mood.

ABOVE AND OPPOSITE Jennifer threads her theme into the master bedroom where a tailored fabric-covered platform holds a luxuriously soft mattress wrapped in striped linen. A salt-and-pepper silk rug leaves the room whisper-quiet and is the perfect spot for a reading chair and footstool. Volumes of sheer fabric can sweep across the view to temper the sun's glare or the city's evening lights.

LONG ISLAND RETREAT

Jennifer's design mission was to take a traditional dark, woody beachside New England interior and bring it to a place of light, fluidity, and relaxed energy, and to provide a showcase where the owners' art collection could shine. The sprawling 10,000-square-foot Hamptons home sits along the beautiful waterway of Mecox Bay, on four acres of manicured land. A lacy curtain of birches filter the sun's rays and provides leafy peeks to the water's edge over a ribbon of verdant pompoms.

It is a place where the owners come with family and friends to escape the city on weekends, though it is in the summer months when it becomes most alive. While the exterior Shingle-Style architecture, so fitting to the Hamptons, remained untouched, Jennifer's interior redesign came to all the surfaces, making for spaces that are alluring, compelling, and modern. From the moment the front door swings open to reveal four contemporary rockers circling a low-slung table, Jennifer set the tone. And it is here, too, where she introduced the distinctive blue that will move through the house like an orchestrated tidal splash.

"THE ROCKING CHAIRS ARE MUCH MORE INVITING AND RECALL THE FRIENDLY SPIRIT OF THE NEW ENGLAND BEACH HOUSES—BUT WITH A TWIST."

Jennifer removed all the dark and honey-toned woods. The white walls and ceilings now show off the architectural details in a new light, and give the rooms a feeling of spaciousness and continuity.

For the floors, she created a custom-stain of heather grey, a color that captures the early morning beach light.

Opting for an uncomplicated color thread of blue and poppy orange that honors the sea, summer sunsets, and garden blooms makes this an easy place to unwind.

Jennifer accomplished her goal to create a chic, comfortable country home that is as easy to be in when it's just for the couple who have come for the weekend, or when the home is brimming with guests on a summer's day.

"IT'S THEIR COUNTRY HOME THAT TURNS INTO THEIR YEAR-ROUND RESORT, AND THAT IS JUST THE FEELING I WAS OUT TO ACHIEVE FOR THEM."

PREVIOUS PAGES The house, by Medford, New York-based Nocera General Contracting, was designed in the classic Shingle-Style of the Hamptons.

OPPOSITE For poolside, Jennifer chose a periwinkle blue Sunbrella fabric to wrap a crescent of easy-back lounge chairs from Royal Botania and accented them with oversized pillows.

OVERLEAF A custom-made wool runner from Doris Leslie Blau, the color of wet beach sand, serves as a pathway to all the rooms.

PAGES 163–166 Four ultra-modern rocking chairs from Poltrona Frau make for an unexpected entry—and are Jennifer's way of declaring her departure from tradition in the Shingle-Style house. The custom-made blue wool rug, edged in leather, also reinforces the color theme.

PREVIOUS PAGES The custom-made coffee table by the Dallas, Texas-based designer Allan Knight nests inside low-rise Minotti sofas set on diagonals. The orange sculpture is by Merete Rasmussen, an artist who shows at the J. Lohmann Gallery, in New York.

ABOVE AND OPPOSITE The formal dining room has been furnished with a table and chairs by Richard Schultz for Knoll. Jennifer chose the overhead lighting from Lasvit because it reminds her of water drops.

OVERLEAF A fifth bedroom became a second-floor family room that gave the boys in the family a place of their own in which to entertain friends. The sea-blue theme was continued here, with chairs from Georgette in a tropical print. The sectional sofa, from Lazzoni, conceals two double beds to accommodate extra guests. The low table provides a great surface for board games.

ARTHUR ELGORT

OPPOSITE AND ABOVE For the master bedroom, the palette of soft blue, lilac, and purple—favorite colors of the clients'—creates a tranquil space. Soft, billowing, translucent custom-made draperies temper the natural fluctuations of light, while framing postcard-perfect water views. The chandelier by designer Natasha Baradaran, from Jean De Merry, reflects the jewel-like, faceted ceiling. In the sunroom off the master bedroom, a coffee table by Jennifer Post Design has been placed between seating by Minotti.

OVERLEAF The blue-and-white theme has been carried right out to the pool and entertainment area where crisp, sculptural furnishings from Royal Botanica, and umbrellas, make for a dramatic visual contrast with the soft shapes of the hydrangea plantings.

PERFECT PANORAMA

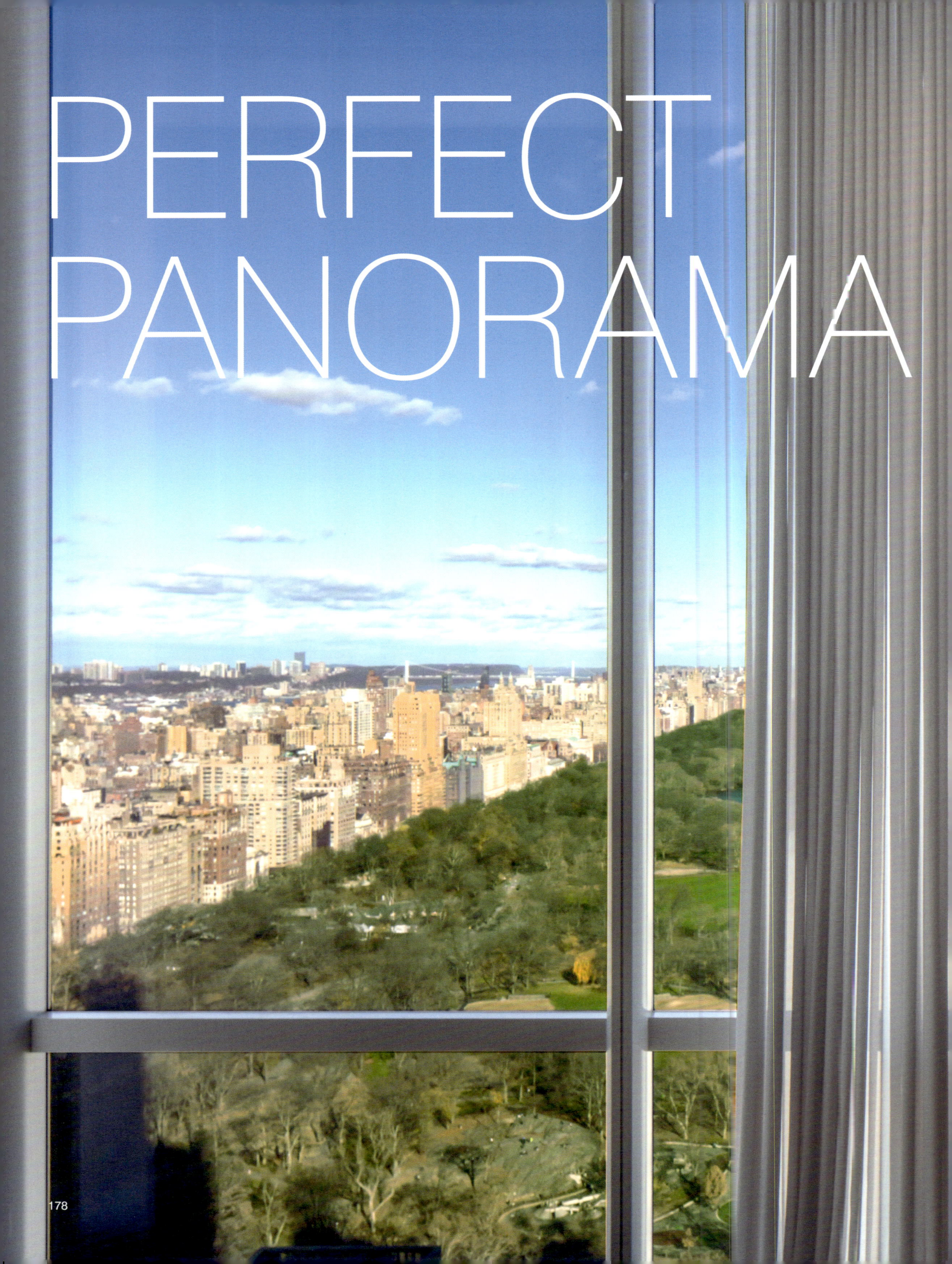

TRENCH
DIANE VON FURSTENBERG
THE LITTLE BLACK DRESS

With her signature design work already in some of the New York's most prestigious luxury high-rises, this commission, at the much-talked-about One57, was one where she could effortlessly go pure Post. Declared the city's tallest residential building four years ago, it is a creation of the French architect Christian de Portzamparc and was built by Gary Barnett of Extell Development. No matter your position in the heart of the city, you will see the 75-story glass sculpture jutting into the skyline. It offers its residents some of the most coveted, breathtaking city views, and this apartment, on the 50th floor, has some of the best.

"IN SUCH A LUXURIOUS SETTING, IT WOULD BE EASY TO OPT FOR GILDING THIS LILY. MY STYLE IS TO JUST SHOW THE LILY IN ITS PUREST FORM. THAT IS WHAT I FEEL I ACCOMPLISHED HERE."

"THE FAMILY WAS FAMILIAR WITH MY WORK AND I WAS TOTALLY DELIGHTED TO HAVE THE OPPORTUNITY TO WORK ON THIS PARTICULAR APARTMENT. WITH VIEWS SMACK IN THE MIDDLE OF CENTRAL PARK—THE DREAM VIEW FOR NEW YORKERS. IT OFFERED ME A SPECIAL CANVAS. THAT THEY COULD ENJOY SUNRISES, SUNSETS, AND VIEWS IN ALL DIRECTIONS, MY FOCUS WAS TO MAKE THAT EVERCHANGING NATURAL ART CENTER STAGE, AND SIMULTANEOUSLY PRESENT A WARM SPACE THAT FELT LIKE HOME."

The 3,500-square-foot apartment serves as a pied-à-terre for the family, who left their residence at the Time Warner Center, opting instead for an address that combined beautiful living space with the ultimate in luxury services. Furnishings in subdued neutral hues are sleek, modern, and purposely low to keep the sweeping views from the floor-to-ceiling windows open to frame blue skies above and the greenery below. Venetian plaster wraps the walls, Jennifer's favorite surface for wicking away glare

"I'VE CREATED INTIMATE SEATING AREAS WHERE THEY CAN GATHER TO TALK, OR HEAD OFF TO CURL UP WITH A BOOK, OR WATCH A MOVIE."

Columns that once interrupted the views were removed, and where Jennifer could extend views even further, she added clean-lined, mirrored columns. Custom built-ins hold an array of art objects and books, and contribute to the "homey" feeling she wanted to achieve.

"THEY COME FROM A VERY LARGE, CLOSE-KNIT FAMILY, AND THIS IS A PLACE WHERE THEY CAN ALL COME AND ENJOY THEIR TIME TOGETHER—HIGH ABOVE THE CITY, IN A RELAXED SETTING."

PREVIOUS PAGES With breathtaking views of Central Park as the focal point, designing the interior of this Manhattan pied-à-terre was the perfect project for Jennifer. Where views were even minimally obstructed, she opened them up and then mapped a floor plan with sophisticated, comfortable furnishings.

OPPOSITE AND OVERLEAF Low, sculpted, snow-white Italian sofas, from Poltrona Frau, flank a glass-topped coffee table, from DDC in New York, in the living room. All are set atop a cloud of the soft pile wool rug from Doris Leslie Blau. Jennifer managed to create the beautiful illusion that this gathering place is simply floating above the city. The metal sculpture by the Canadian artist Martha Sturdy rises gently off the table's center point. The table was a custom-made piece by Jennifer and the American designer Paul Ferrante. Jennifer introduced a pop of color and texture with the maroon beeswax piece by the New York-based artist LeRone Wilson.

A trio of tear-drop chandeliers in copper and silver tones add a bit of contrast and whimsy. The dining area aligns visually with the coal-black detailing of the living room.

CHANEL
THE SCHOOL OF FASHION

PREVIOUS PAGES Jennifer used every opportunity to create gathering places for the family. This one, in the living room, with its three comfy swivel chairs from the Swiss company de Sede, offers just that, along with a perfect setting to look at television. The glass-topped table's angular base plays off the curves of the chairs.

OPPOSITE AND ABOVE In a departure from a neutral palette, Jennifer designed this guest bedroom in shades of green that recall the views of the treetops in Central Park. To further anchor the theme, she wrapped the walls in an earth-toned grass cloth. Her choice of silk fabrics for the bedcover and pillows reminds us of the park's variegated textures and plantings, as does the wall art by Brendan Burns, a Welsh artist. The platform bed seems to float (and aptly so) atop a snow-white Doris Leslie Blau silk ridged rug, perhaps a metaphor for a Central Park stream.

THE OTHER WHITE HOUSE

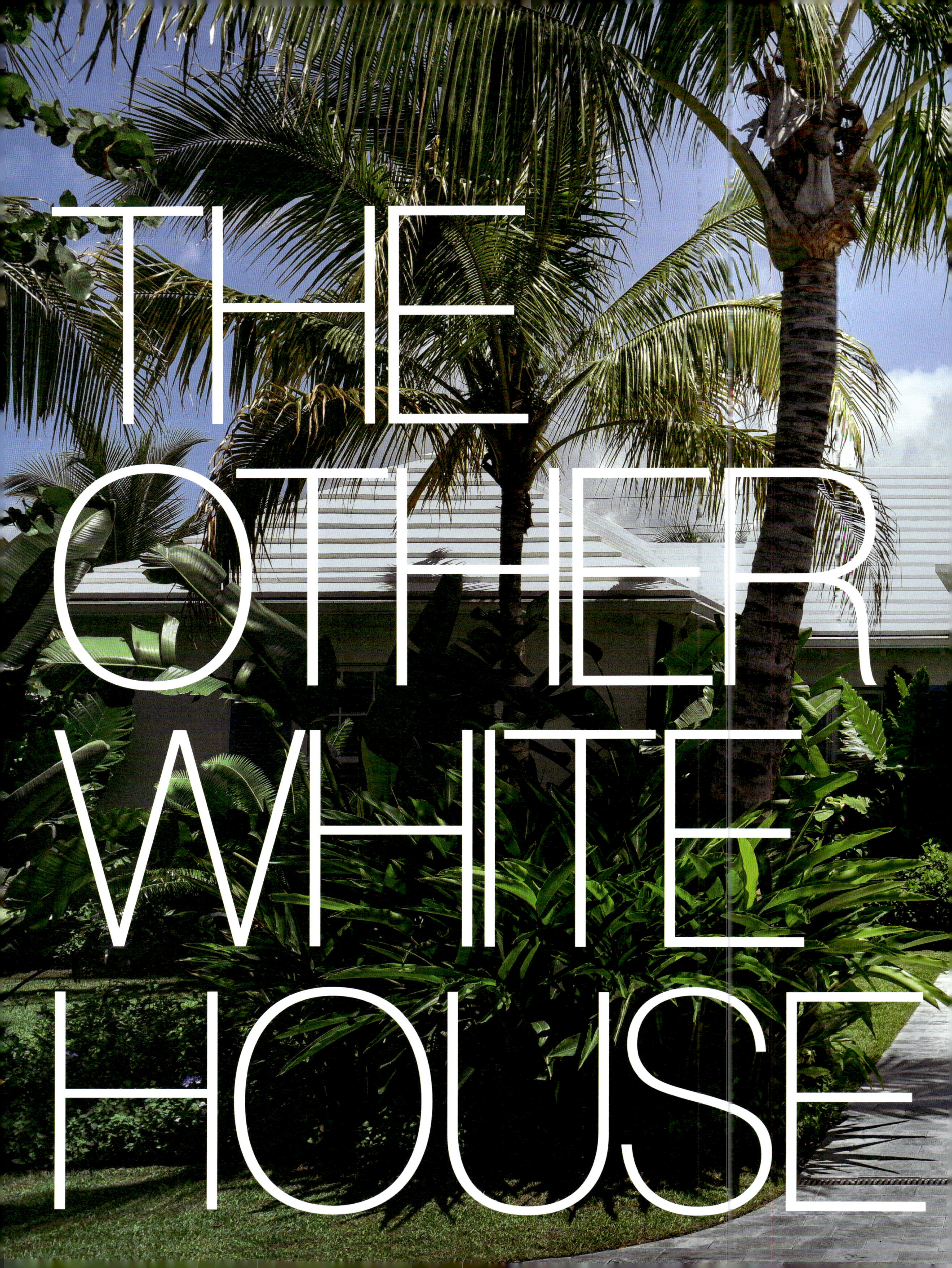

"BECAUSE THEY BOTH LIVE AND WORK HERE, IT WAS IMPORTANT TO ME TO CREATE SPACE WHERE THEY COULD MOVE FROM WORK TO ENTERTAINING TO RELAXING, IN EASY, NATURAL TRANSITIONS."

When the call came in to Jennifer's office from this Palm Beach, Florida, couple, you could say the design stars had aligned. They were hoping to meet with her and discuss their New York condominium. As it was during Christmas break, Jennifer was coincidentally in Palm Beach, and the meeting was quickly arranged. The husband, famous for his business acumen running companies that have come to define American culture, and she, with a successful career in the designer building industry, were soon sitting with Jennifer and describing their vision for their new Florida home, instead of their Manhattan residence.

"THEY HAD BEEN RENTING ON THIS STREET, AND WHEN THIS LOT BECAME AVAILABLE, THEY PURCHASED IT, TORE DOWN THE RANCH, AND BEGAN PLANNING. AS THEY SPOKE, ALL KINDS OF IDEAS WERE COMING TO MIND, AND I SHARED THEM IN THIS VERY IMPROMPTU PRESENTATION! BY THAT EVENING, WE WERE WORKING TOGETHER."

John, who was raised in Bermuda, has a special affection for the island's architecture and began tapping into Jennifer's "design mine" for imaginative ways to honor the character of the island.

John and the West Palm Beach-based architectural firm Smith & Moore's concept for the entry that recalled the architecture of the island's old butteries further inspired Jennifer. And so the design story and a bit of John's story began, as all good stories do, right at the front door.

The stepped roof dovetails with the main roof, and the plantation-style front door begins an island theme that weaves thoughout the rooms.

Step inside the front door and the entrance foyer is as cool as the buttery concept. A grey, pebble-tiled floor and concrete bench anchor what is a casual, functional space.

"THIS AND DETAILS LIKE THE PLANTATION SHUTTER-STYLE WALL TAKES HIS ISLAND HISTORY HOME TO CONTINUE HIS LIFE STORY. IT GAVE ME GREAT SATISFACTION TO BE ABLE TO DO THAT. IT WAS AN EXHILARATING, EXCITING CREATIVE PROCESS."

Furnishings and colors tell an uncomplicated story in white, blue, and grey. It is a place where comfort and a lightness of being reign.

"CAPTURING THE LUSH, BEAUTIFUL VIEWS OF SURROUNDING GREENERY IN AN OPEN, LIGHT-FILLED SPACE WAS ANOTHER MUST THAT IS ALWAYS ON MY DESIGN RADAR."

PREVIOUS PAGES The interiors of the Bermuda-style home in Palm Beach, Florida were designed by Jennifer. The stepped roof, so familiar in the architecture of Bermuda, recalls the owner's roots, and set the stage for an interior that continues his story.

OPPOSITE Jennifer complemented the entry with pebble-stone tiles, a plantation-style door, and ceiling lighting that is reminiscent of the island's traditional hand fans.

OPPOSITE AND ABOVE In continuing the island theme, Jennifer designed a plantation-style shutter wall for the living room that backlights the adjacent staircase to the second-floor bedroom level. The painting, *The Pedestrians*, by the American artist James Zwadlo, breaks up the sea of white.

OVERLEAF Delicate basket-weave style chair legs surround a glass-topped table, encouraging light to bathe all corners of the room. Jennifer added a large window that framed a custom-made waterfall to provide an engaging, meditative focus where the spouse practices her morning yoga.

PREVIOUS PAGES Dramatic grey-veined Carrara marble that wraps the countertops, the backsplash, and the shelving adds visual interest to Jennifer's signature white custom lacquer finishes in this pristine, modern space.

RIGHT For the master bedroom, her choice of blues moved back on the spectrum to the palest hue, very much like dawn's morning summer sky. An organic wallpaper from China Seas envelopes the room in a garden pattern, and a matching blue silk rug sits beneath the soft upholstered bed.

PAGES 200–203 Jennifer's design theme was carried poolside. With fabrics in a mix of solids and leaf prints, her choice provides a subtle cue of entry from inside to outside in a seamless, welcoming, and understated fashion.

SCIENCE BUSINESS

DOWNTOWN GLAMOUR

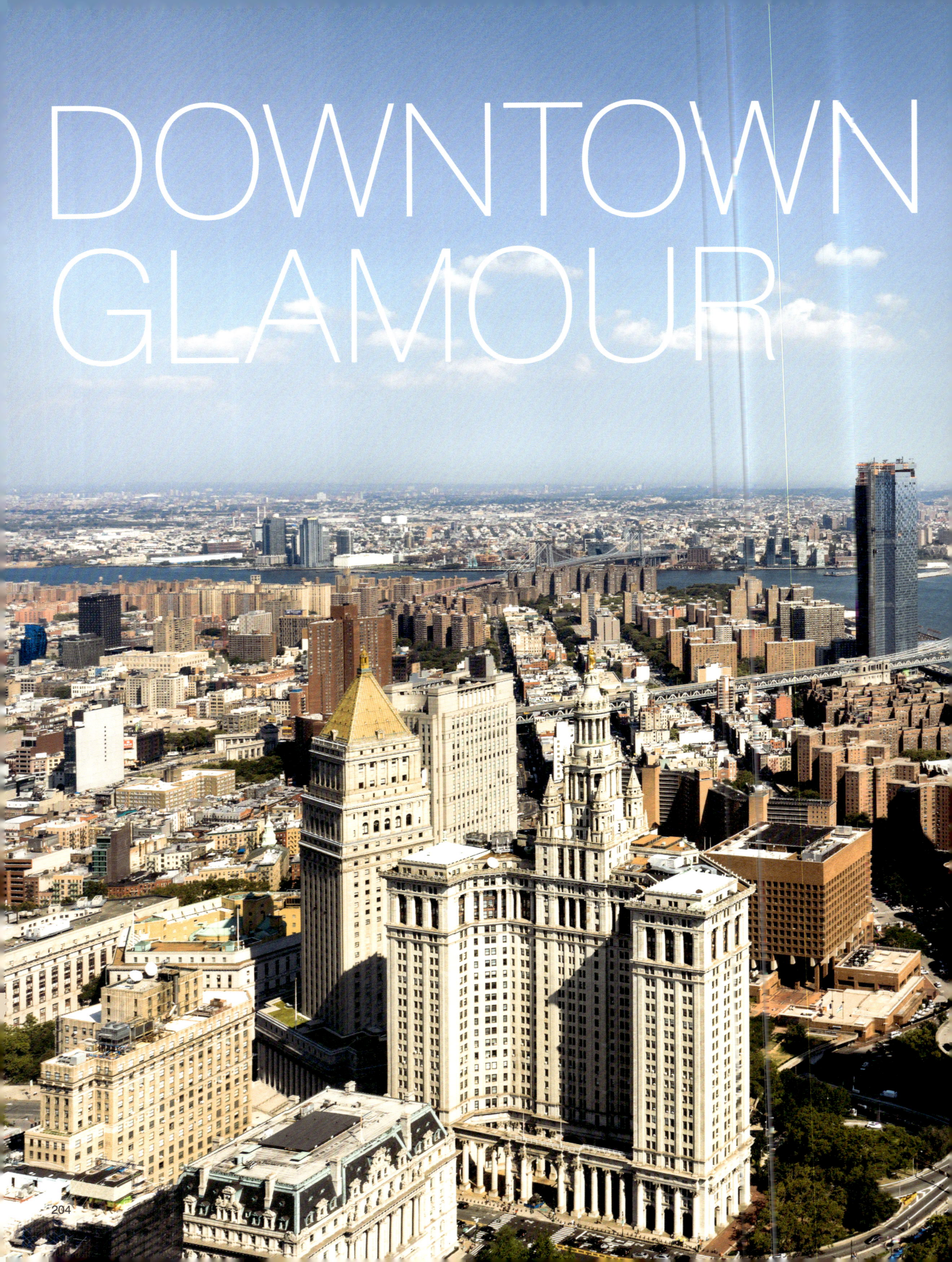

"IT WAS A WONDERFUL OPPORTUNITY TO CREATE A COMFORTABLE, ELEGANT HOME. THERE IS NOTHING TRENDY HERE AND FURNISHINGS ARE NOT DEFINED AS ITALIAN OR MODERN. MY GOAL WAS TO DESIGN ORIGINAL PIECES THAT FIT THE MOOD AND THE FUNCTION, WHICH WERE ART FORMS IN THEIR OWN RIGHT, AND THAT MADE FOR A DRAMATIC DIALOGUE BETWEEN LIGHT, COLOR, AND TEXTURE."

With their children grown, the couple, both attorneys, moved to the city, where they would be closer to their law firm and all that they enjoy in Manhattan after work. Their newly designed home-to-be: a penthouse on the 76th floor at the much-talked about Robert A.M. Stern-designed Four Seasons Hotel and Residences. With huge expanses of windows, its stunning panoramic city views map the city's architectural history and bathe the space in one of Jennifer's favorite design elements—natural light. At 7,800 square feet, it is a spacious home, and one that gave Jennifer an unusual artistic opportunity. The couple's art collection, including a collection of glass in a rainbow of jewel-like colors, also inspired her to adopt an unexpected palette.

"THEY ARE JOYFUL, HAPPY PEOPLE WHO LOVE COLOR. HERE, COLOR IS DANCING EVERYWHERE. ROOM TO ROOM, I'VE LINKED A THREAD OF RELATED TONES. WHILE EACH ROOM'S DESIGN AND FURNISHINGS ARE DISTINCT, I ALSO WANTED THERE TO BE THIS SUBTLE, ENGAGING FAMILIARITY."

All her furnishing designs have soft, rounded, sculptural edges that recall the gracious architectural curves she created for the entry vestibule, and where she built shelving to showcase their glass collection.

"THIS SET THE MOOD FOR WHAT CONTINUES AS UPLIFTING, HAPPY SPACE—QUALITIES SO TRUE TO THE OWNERS."

For the 10- by 25-foot living room, Jennifer lowered ceilings and divided the space into two distinct seating areas—one with two couches and the other with a low table surrounded by club chairs.

"I WANTED THIS SPACE TO BE MORE INTIMATE AND BREAK IT INTO CONVERSATION AREAS. I FIND MORE AND MORE PEOPLE ENJOY SITTING AND EATING IN THEIR LIVING ROOMS. IT LOOKS MUCH LIKE THE TEA TABLES YOU SEE IN HOTELS WHERE PEOPLE COME TOGETHER FOR INTIMATE LUNCHES AND CONVERSATION."

A color scheme of arctic-white with pops of deep, rich tangerine infused the kitchen with the spouse's favorite color. For the library, warm lemon yellow makes for inviting space "whether with a book or a cocktail in hand."

"FOR THE MASTER BEDROOM, I INTRODUCED THE PALEST OF CELERY AND A YELLOW THAT IS NEARLY BONE—SUBTLE TONES THAT TIE THE HOUSE TOGETHER, BUT HERE, COLOR WAS TONED FOR TRANQUILITY, A PLACE YOU CAN FEEL THE DAY WIND DOWN."

PREVIOUS PAGES The panoramic views from this 76th floor Manhattan penthouse define drama.

OPPOSITE Club chairs from J. Robert Scott in New York, upholstered in velvet with silver-metal-banded arms, hug a tea table and provide an intimate seating area just beyond the foyer. Jennifer chose a celadon green silk rug with an embossed rectangle pattern from Doris Leslie Blau to distinguish the area.

ABOVE Jennifer's build-out of a half-moon wall presents as a welcoming, elegant space. The diminishing width of the built-in shelf accentuates the curve while leading us into the home. The painting, entitled *Lawyer*, is by the Colombian artist Fernando Botero.

OPPOSITE The couple's extraordinary collection of colorful contemporary glass is displayed in custom-built cubbies, each sized to accommodate the shapes of the individual objects. Tiny strategically placed spotlights allow the cuts and colors to shine museum-style.

OVERLEAF Soft grey and white furnishings, all from J. Robert Scott, except for the grey chairs by Dakota Jackson, contrast with artwork in rich shades of maroon and blue. The bronze and wood bench titled *Angel Chair* by the American artist Wendell Castle weaves an organic shape into the space. *The Dance*, a sculpture by the Ukrainian-born American artist Alexander Archipenko, atop a lacquered wooden base, separates two distinct seating areas in the open living room. The portrait of *Pia Zadora* is by the American Pop Art artist Andy Warhol.

ABOVE Jennifer inserted a clean-lined, contemporary fireplace flush to the wall, serving as an organic, flame-fed sculpture, framed in bands of steel.

OPPOSITE Ultra-plush upholstered seating picks up on the colors in the canvas *Untitled* by the American artist Sam Francis. The glass-topped coffee table is a Jennifer Post design.

BVLGARI
ROMA

OPPOSITE When the pocket doors dividing the rooms are slid back, new views of the city and sky can open up the space. For candlelit, quiet dinners, they slide back to create an intimate, more romantic room.

ABOVE The colorful 1958 canvas titled *Heat* by the American artist Kenneth Noland is mirrored in the metal bands of the chairs, taking the art into what appears to be a fabric pattern.

OVERLEAF Marshmallow-white leather chairs surround a lacquer table like a grouping of clouds floating above a soft, low-pile silk rug. *Harlequin*, a whimsical clock by Wendell Castle, with a flame-like brass hour hand, plays off the high-rise verticals in the view. Jennifer's sleek, custom-made sideboard holds all that's needed to set an elegant dinner table. A colorful canvas by Kenneth Noland adds warmth to the room and recalls the thread of primary colors in other rooms. The silver candlesticks on the table are part of the Cobra collection by Constantin Wortmann for Georg Jensen.

OPPOSITE Two pieces of tangerine glass flank a stack of handmade bowls on shelving of the same hue and create a pleasing vignette. Below, a white porcelain pitcher and a porcelain sculpture by the American ceramic artist Anna Kasabian await fresh ingredients from the kitchen.

ABOVE In her quest to remind us that nature's creatures are both beautiful and soothing, Jennifer introduced two cranes-a'calling to the work surface—perhaps as a subtle reminder to balance work with a walk in the park.

OVERLEAF In the spirit of the dawning of a new day, Jennifer moved the cheer of tangerine touches through the kitchen with solids and weaves on slim, contour-fitting chairs, an expanse of tangerine on the drawer tops, a cushy underfoot rug, and upward to a light fixture by the American glass artist Darren Goodman. It is a place where the tasks of cooking, watching the news with coffee, and catching up with emails come together in one light-filled spot. Jennifer kept the look clean and contemporary, with cabinetry that is set back from the view but also has enough visual variety in cubbies, shelving, and cabinets to be interesting. Her clever use of backlighting on the main wall of cabinetry transforms it into a free-form sculptural event.

WARHOL

ART FLYING

RIGHT In a departure from neutrals and white, Jennifer created an outside-the-design-box library in a multitude of yellow hues that move from deep sunflower to the palest hue on the scale. With the yellow rug as its core, and movement out to seating and walls, we are reminded of the way velvety flower petals open to the sun. With an eye to encouraging longer stays, she chose fabrics and buttery leathers for the upholstery—temptresses to hold a book longer, or let time just pass. Wispy yards of silk can sweep across the patio doors and temper the light.

OVERLEAF A multi-colored nature-themed canvas—*The Pond*—by the American artist Richard Pousette-Dart anchors the tranquil mood of the master bedroom. Jennifer played off the painting's green hue and introduced the palest shades of celery to surround the room. Twin, two-tone custom cabinets, also her design, while functional, are signature pieces as elegant, sculpted works of art.

LIVING IN STYLE AMSTERDAM
FLOWERS ART & BOUQUETS

OPPOSITE A simple glass-base lamp rests on the custom-made nightstand that features a stone top and open storage.

ABOVE A hand-carved wooden light by Wendell Castle, appropriately by the window, seems to recall a bird in flight, and offers additional warmth and texture to a sunny corner.

OVERLEAF In the evening, Jennifer's wide, curved entry provides a kaleidoscopic view into the chic living room.

PAGES 230–231 When the sky turns ink-black, the twinkling city lights appear like a sequined fabric unfurling along the horizon. It is a place where the interior merges with the outside in a heavenly collaboration.

ethos
WATER
INTERIOR DESIGN DOCUMENTS
DESIGN DEVELOPMENT SET
MICHAEL DAVIS CONSTRUCTION, INC.
JENNIFER POST, INC.
326 OCEAN ROAD
326 OCEAN RD.
BRIDGEHAMPTON, NEW
INTERIOR ELEVATION - BATH 1 NORTH WALL
BATH 1 EAST WALL (SHOWER INTERIOR)

BANGKOK

 Antoine Bootz: 10-11, 16-17, 19-27, 30-87, 102-126, 128-131, 204-231. Pieter Estersohn: 134-137, 140-141, 144-145. Matt Fargo: 132-133, 138-139, 142-143. Scott Frances: 90-101. Photography by Ken Hayden: opposite title page, 5, 188-203. Pete Krasowski: 146-157, 178-186. Rick Lew: 187. Michael Moran: 13, 18, 28-29, 158-177. Timothy Schenck: 88-89.

COVER The coal-black sculpture, *Standing Bronze #7,* by Honolulu-based artist John Koga, from Ralph Pucci, plays off the hard-edged border of architecture in the mapped streetscape below the spectacular sky-high New York penthouse designed by Jennifer Post.

ENDPAPERS Jennifer inspected a barn door she had custom-made for a penthouse in Miami, Florida.

BACK OF FRONT ENDPAPERS Evening is one of Jennifer's favorite times of day to walk on the beach in Palm Beach, Florida.

OPPOSITE TITLE PAGE Jennifer stood proudly in front of a newly completed project in Palm Beach, Florida.

PAGE 4 "Being on site is the only way to make sure it's happening," explained Jennifer on the progress of the construction of a home in Los Angeles, California.

PAGE 5 Jennifer was photographed after finishing a penthouse in Miami, Florida.

CONTENTS Of a project in the Caribbean, Jennifer exclaimed: "It doesn't get more rewarding than this … pure joy."

PAGE 9 Visiting Vietnam, Jennifer explored the local sites by boat.

PAGE 232 Jennifer worked onsite on a project in Bridgehampton, New York.

PAGE 233 Jennifer paused while exploring Bangkok, Thailand, on foot.

OPPOSITE Travel is a big part of Jennifer's life. Clockwise from top left, she was visiting Thailand on the coast of Puglia, Italy; taking a break from hiking in Europe; meeting a dancer after a performance in Thailand; playing with local children on the street in Tanzania; smiling brightly on a dock in Vietnam; spotting a zebra on safari in Kenya; and on a bike trip in South Africa.

PAGE 238 CLOCKWISE FROM TOP The team at Jennifer Post Design, *from the left,* Smith McLean, Harpreet Sia, Jennifer Post, Franco Rivera, Lena Kravtsova, and Motoki Asaoka; Jennifer's parents, RoseAnn and Jack Post, happily visiting her on site in Los Angeles, California; Jennifer with Franco Rivera, the director of the company.

BACK OF BACK ENDPAPERS Jennifer enjoyed the natural light in a recently finished project in Miami, Florida.

BANGKOK

THANK YOU

To my family, for always loving and supporting me.

To my wonderful staff who are brilliant each in their own way and amazingly talented: Lena Kravtsova, Franco Rivera, Motoki Asaoka, Smith McLean, Kyle Weeks and Harpreet Sial. A very special appreciation and love for Lena, who has grown my business with me from the beginning.

Thank you to all of my incredible clients for letting me express myself and have the freedom to create limitlessly and with so much passion. I cannot thank you enough from the bottom of my heart.

Thank you to:

Larry Korman, you're amazing, talented, and a dear dear friend.

John Hannan, an amazing man, an amazing client and an amazing friend.

Paige Rense, thank you for believing in me and for starting my career.

My brilliant publisher Pointed Leaf Press, Suzanne Slesin, Publisher, who was also instrumental in starting my career. And to the creative director, Carlos Frederico Farina, and managing editor, Kelly Koester for giving me a wonderful book.

Pamela Jaccarino, the great editor of Luxe.

Thank you also to the wonderful photographers who made my second monograph possible: Ken Hayden, Michael Moran, Antoine Bootz, and Peter Krakowski.

Joseph Hertzberg, a beautiful friend who has always been there for me.

Anna Kasabian—I love you, dear friend.

My Beautiful God Parents: Betty Terry, Billy & Jim Maynard.

Raymond Lu and his family at Centerline Management for always executing my vision with perfection.

My first-class contractors Highline Construction, SilverLining, Michael Davis Construction and Total Home.

Ralph Pucci, who is a close friend of mine and an incredible curator.

Michael Zenreich: Thank you so much, always.

Martin and Dorothy at KGM, the incredibly talented lighting designers.

Aucapina Cabinets, and their family, for their dedication to their craft, and their love and support.

Vicky Gorelik at Windows Walls & More, and her fabulous team that executes the finest upholstery in their field.

My dear friend Kay Handman.

Susan Izsak at Doris Leslie Blau for the years of friendship and for helping me bring my designs to life.

Michael Merritt and Merritt Woodworking.

David Floricic at ProDesign, who is a longtime friend—the best stone trade in the business.

Audio Command Systems: Tom Clancy, you are the best.

My dear friend Gregory Marshall at J. Robert Scott, whom I have known since the beginning of my career. Thank you for being yourself and for your incredible eye for beauty.

Kim Collins and Amy Morgenstern, of Kamp Studios, who both mean so much to me. They are the best plaster workers in the city, and true artists.

My friends, Eren Uster and Efe Kababulut, at Lazzoni, whom I have known for years, thank you.

The beautiful Hakakian family and Myrna Corliss at DDC, who have been essential in bringing my designs to life.

Jan Pesce at Mark Phillips: Thank you for years of business and friendship.

Regina Bilotta, a dear friend and first-class kitchen manufacturer.

Brian Furr at Poliform: Thank you for your devotion to your craft.

Olivier Giugni for always inspiring me with your chic floral arrangements. You're a true artist and friend.

Karen Comerford, a dear friend of mine with the best design boutique in the Hamptons.

The fabulous Daniel Volpa at Patterson Flynn & Martin, who is always so stylish and an incredible person.

Carol Swedlow at Aronson's: Thank you so many years of collaboration.

Alyssa Cohen at California Closets—we have had so much fun working together all of these years.

Eric Slayton, the master of concrete.

Patrick Matthew Smyth, a longtime mentor.

Caryn Schacht and Tom Lampson at Lorin Marsh, thank you.

Scalamandré, the premier fabric house.

Brett Beldock and Teri Lebow, my dear friends and fellow designers, thank you.

Freddy Almonte, the resident manager at One57, an incredible man who manages one of the greatest building in New York City.

John Koga: You are truly an incredible artist.

Robert Kuo, an amazing artist and true inspiration.

Nico Yektai, a true artist of custom furniture.

Douglas Fanning, my longtime friend and amazing artist in the metal world.

Mark Humphrey, a longtime friend and incredible artist.

Ned Rabrenovic at Capital City Movers.

Julia Foster at Luxury Living.

Marders

Julie and Royce Pinkwater, and Gabrielle at Pinkwater Select.

Sabrina Fierman and Little Elves

John Simone, my wonderful lawyer.

Sam Rein, my incredible accountant.

And to Annabelle, my dear, sweet Boston Terrier.

–Jennifer Post, New York, March 2019

JENNIFER POST is the mastermind and driving force behind the award-winning architecture and New York-based design firm, Jennifer Post Design (www.JenniferPostDesign.com). For over 20 years, Jennifer has been at the forefront of creating elegantly modern, contemporary homes with the flair of sophistication sought by her following of elite clientele. Post's ability to edit down living spaces to the most essential, uncluttered luxuries has earned her and her firm a world-class reputation amongst the country's leading architects and designers.

ANNA KASABIAN is a freelance writer, journalist, and author of 15 books—twelve on interior design and architecture, and three cookbooks. Her work as a porcelain artist (www.AnnaKasabianPorcelain.com) is an extension of her passion for design.

Her articles have been published in regional and national magazines including *Architectural Digest*, *Luxe*, *Metropolitan Home*, *The Robb Report*, *Coastal Living*, and *USA Today*, among many others. She has lectured on interior design, and appeared on HGTV.

PUBLISHER/EDITORIAL DIRECTOR **SUZANNE SLESIN**
CREATIVE DIRECTOR **FREDERICO FARINA**
MANAGING EDITOR **KELLY KOESTER**
PRINTED IN ITALY
FIRST EDITION
ISBN: 978-1-938461-88-0
LOC: 2019902814

Pointed Leaf Press, LLC., 136 Baxter Street, Suite 1C, New York, NY 10013. www.pointedleafpress.com